PROJECT ECO-CITY

YOUR WILD NEIGHBOURHOOD

PHILIP PARKER

Wayland

PROJECT ECO-CITY

Your Living Home
Your Wild Neighbourhood
Town Life
Global Cities

This book was prepared for Wayland (Publishers) Ltd by
Globe Education, Nantwich, Cheshire

Concept design and artwork by SPL Design

Cover picture: Red squirrel

First published in 1994 by
Wayland (Publishers) Ltd
61 Western Road, Hove
East Sussex, BN3 1JD, England

Printed and bound by
G. Canale & C. S. p. A., Turin

British Library Cataloguing in Publication Data
Parker, Philip
Your Wild Neighbourhood. – (Project
Eco-city Series)
I. Title II. Series
574.5268

ISBN 0 7502 1305 1

Picture acknowledgements:
Biophoto Associates 13
Bruce Coleman *cover* (Gordon Langsbury), 8 (Jose Luis Gonzales Grande), 9l (George McCarthy),
31 (Jane Burton), 39 (Joy Langsbury)
Ecoscene 4l (Nigel Hawkes), 5b, 20, 21 (David Purslow), 23 (David Purslow), 24, 26, 35r, 37m (Ian Harwood), 37b, 41, 44l
Heather Angel 4t (Jason Venus), 5l, 6t, 16, 19t, 22, 25b (Andrew Henley), 30t (Jason Venus), 33b, 37t, 38, 42t, 45t
NHPA 5tr (John Shaw), 6b (E A Janes), 9r (David Woodfall), 12 (Stephen Dalton), 14 (Stephen Dalton),
17 (Stephen Dalton), 18 (M. I. Garwood), 19b (Stephen Dalton), 30b (Michael Leach), 34 (Laurie Campbell),
35l (Stephen Dalton), 40 (Stephen Dalton), 42b (Stephen Dalton), 43t (Michael Leach),
44r (Andy Rouse), 45l (Michael Leach)
OSF 10 (Harry Fox), 11 (David Thompson), 43b (Geoff Kidd)
Sutton Grammar School Conservation Club 28, 29
Tony Stone 32 (D. C. Lowe)
Wayland Picture Library 23
Zefa 26, 33t, 36

Contents

Beyond your doorstep

Next time you are out and about in your neighbourhood – stop and shut your eyes. Listen: how many different sounds can you hear? Can you tell what each one is? Smell: breathe in through your nose. Try to describe the smells in words. Look: open your eyes and look down and then up above you. What life do you see?

A fox cub in the suburbs of a city.

Even in the heart of a city a wall may bloom into life.

At first it may seem that your neighbourhood has little non-human life. But if you look, you will find grasses and mosses growing between stone and asphalt, beetles and birds in trees, butterflies and bees on flowers, and even squirrels in parks.

There will be many 'habitats' near you. Think of the great lengths of walls, roads and pavements in your neighbourhood, the ponds or lakes that may be nearby, wastelands and cemeteries, parks and railway lines. Now think of how many habitats there must be in your town – and how many towns and cities there are in your country. It is no wonder that some creatures, such as frogs and bees, thrive better in towns than in the fast disappearing countryside.

Starlings flying into the centre of London to roost overnight.

An opossum in a US garden.

These neighbourhood habitats are continually changing. Plants and animals grow, leaves change colour and the numbers of creatures rise and fall. Animals go through changes as they grow and everything is feeding on or being eaten by something else.

A kookaburra – the Australian kingfisher.

Your neighbourhood is also changed by other parts of the city. Wind blows the seeds of weeds and trees to a local garden or wasteland. Roads, railways and canals bring in plants and animals from hundreds of kilometres away. Your local lake may attract birds that have flown thousands of kilometres. When you step beyond your doorstep you enter a very busy – and changing – world. You will need all your senses to explore it.

City canyons

Think of a built-up part of your town or city and you probably think of busy pavements and roads underfoot, and tall buildings overhead. Can only humans live here?

In even the busiest city centres there are plants in flower beds, tubs and window boxes. But they play a very small part in city life. The 'empty' pavements, roads, backyards and 'vacant lots' are very important. They are mini-canyons, each with many mini-habitats.

Perhaps the harshest environment is the pavement on which we walk. Only algae and lichens can live here, hugging the surface in a crust. But even these can be killed by pollution and the trampling of humans. Between the paving slabs are thin ribbons of soil which provide a good base for dandelions and thistles, and 'escaped' plants from gardens. These plants can thrive close to the wall, sheltered from trampling feet.

It's not just human feet that create a problem. Pavements heat up during the day, so creatures such as slugs, earthworms and centipedes hide underneath where it is cool. At night, the slabs lose their heat and become colder than the air. Moisture collects on the cold slabs and the creatures emerge to feed.

The key to the dandelion's success is that its light seeds can be blown long distances.

When burdock flowers ripen, seeds grow. These seeds have many sharp hooks. The seeds hook on to passing animals and are carried away.

rosebay willowherb →

wallflower →

moth →

slug

shepherd's purse

dandelion

groundsel

ants

greater plantain

ground beetle

earthworm

rye grass

Life on the streets.

Trees bring relief!

Have you ever noticed that the base of some street trees are darker in colour than the rest of the trunk? This is particularly common when trees are by the entrances to parks. These patches are mats of dark green algae. The remainder of the trunk has lighter green algae or lichen. Dark algae are encouraged by the rich nutrients contained in dog urine. Scientists call this part of a tree the 'canine zone'.

As well a being prone to trampling, many city plants face a problem with reproduction. There may not be another member of the same species nearby for pollination, and there may not be another suitable site for a plant to grow. The most successful pavement plants, such as the dandelion, pollinate themselves and produce seeds that are carried by the wind.

City cliffs

For the wildlife that lives in them, city centres are rather like cliffs. This is especially true for birds. Many species have given up rock faces and adapted to buildings. Pigeons, kestrels, starlings, sparrows, swifts and even gulls have moved into the built-up towns.

A kestrel will find a good place to watch for prey.

In London 600 years ago, people first wrote about pigeons setting up colonies. The pigeon's ancestors were wild rock doves who lived on cliffs nesting in crevices and caves. Today, pigeons thrive on buildings with ledges for roosting, and nesting places inside. They are not as strong as their wild relatives, but they have thicker bills to cope with a larger range of food.

In towns the two most common species are the feral pigeon and the wood pigeon (the word feral means 'wild'). Large numbers of these birds live together in towns, but they do not compete for the same food and living space. Feral pigeons prefer streets, squares and small green spaces; wood pigeons prefer trees, shrubs and large open spaces and eat the berries, buds and leaves they find there. Feral pigeons, on the other hand, rely much more on food scraps thrown away by humans.

City centres support huge numbers of dozens of different bird species. Some of these attract birds of prey. The kestrel has adapted to the human cliffs of our cities. It is quite at home nesting in church towers, high-rise blocks, factory roofs, cranes and pylons. In the wild, the kestrel eats small mammals like voles as well as insects. In the town, it eats mostly small birds, particularly sparrows.

The wild pigeon — one of the most
common street birds anywhere.

A stork's nest, added to each year,
can sometimes build up to 2 m in diameter.

SURVEY OF BIRDS AND THEIR HABITATS

Choose a quiet street to study town birds and see how many
different places there are for birds to feed and rest.
Draw a chart like the one shown below listing all these places.

	road	gutter	pavement	trees	bushes	grass	buildings	sky
house sparrow								
tree sparrow								
hedge sparrow								
pigeon								
robin								
blackbird								
starling								
house martin								
blue tit								

The best times to
study birds are in
the morning or late
afternoon – many
rest in the middle
of the day.

You may need a bird
identification book.
Walk along the street
quietly and look for
birds. As you see each
kind, write its name
on your chart and add
a tick to show where
you saw it.

Camp followers

Ever since humans first began to build villages and towns, wildlife has followed them and adapted to the new environment. The most successful followers are the birds. And the birds themselves bring many unwanted guests – both plants and animals.

Most town authorities are allowed to kill birds such as starlings, house sparrows and pigeons because they carry many pests and diseases. Pigeons carry a yeast fungus which is present in their droppings – and can survive for many years. It can lead to the serious disease called meningitis in humans – each year about 250 people in the USA catch this disease from pigeons.

These beetles are carried by birds and live in their nests. Once the birds leave, the beetles go in search of food.

Starlings were first taken into the USA in 1890 and today have spread to almost every city. They carry a fungus which grows in soil containing bird and bat droppings and which can give humans a disease. A troop of Boy Scouts who cleared a park in Missouri, USA, all caught this disease, as well as the people who lived in a building where the air conditioner drew in air over a pile of starling droppings. The fungi also grow in birds' nests, which are home to dozens of tiny creatures. Since pigeons and sparrows nest inside buildings they can bring with them many beetles, mites and fleas.

Mammals are less adaptable to city life than birds or beetles. The brown rat, house mouse and feral cat are the most successful town-living mammals.

Perhaps one quarter of a town's cats are strays. London alone has about 500,000 stray cats, relying on humans for 75 per cent of their diet – scraps put out for them. Most of the rest comes from scavenging garbage. Cats especially kill a lot of creatures which they do not eat. Pet cats take to their owners a wide range of kills – mostly sparrows, but some mice, rats and beetles, and even the occasional frog!

Cat and mouse – the rodent is safe for the moment!

MAP YOUR NEIGHBOURHOOD HABITATS

A habitat map is a good way to find out about your neighbourhood. You may be able to buy or borrow various maps of your town and neighbourhood, or make a copy of them. Then you can add your notes and draw in the areas of interest.

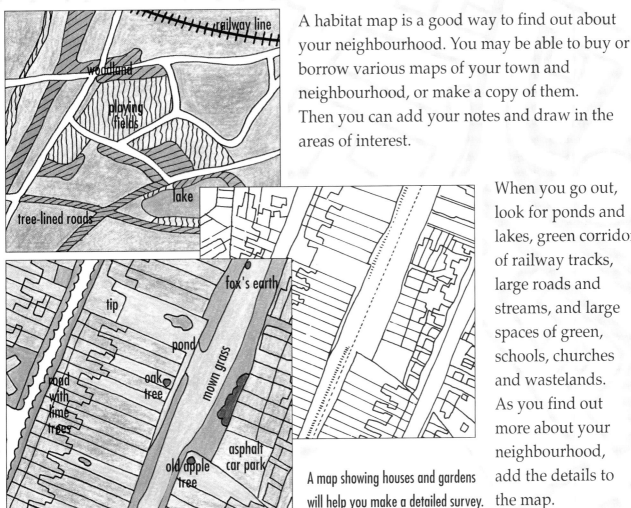

When you go out, look for ponds and lakes, green corridors of railway tracks, large roads and streams, and large spaces of green, schools, churches and wastelands. As you find out more about your neighbourhood, add the details to the map.

A map showing houses and gardens will help you make a detailed survey.

Pond life

The local pond or lake teems with plant and animal life. For example, the lakes of New York's Central Park are believed to hold 3,000,000,000,000,000,000 living things!

As many country ponds are destroyed, the still waters of towns become vital for wildlife. A pond in a garden or school is usually small and shallow, lined with plastic or concrete, and topped up with tap water. But even this 'unnatural' environment can become an important habitat. One in ten gardens in Britain has a pond.

The surface of a pond is covered in a 'film' which can hold animals like pond skaters.

Tiny plants soon grow on the surface of a new pond. They use the sun's energy to help make food from nutrients in the water. The plants reproduce rapidly and soon the water is thick with them, providing food for many other animals. Midges will visit to lay their eggs, water boatmen and pond skaters will fly in, and water snails hatch out. Frogs and toads will soon find the pond to breed in.

Ponds in parks are often very different from those in gardens. Most are supplied by a nearby stream, and they usually have more nutrients washed into them which encourages more plant growth. The numbers of fish can be quite large and include roach, perch and carp. Goldfish, originally from Asia, are often put into ponds. They are very hardy and can survive the winter cold. Sometimes they become green – their natural wild colour.

The pond environment is fairly stable: there are no strong currents and the temperature of the water doesn't change as much as the temperature of the air. If the temperature does fall to freezing point and the water starts to ice over, some fish sink to the bottom of the pond and hibernate in the mud until the spring.

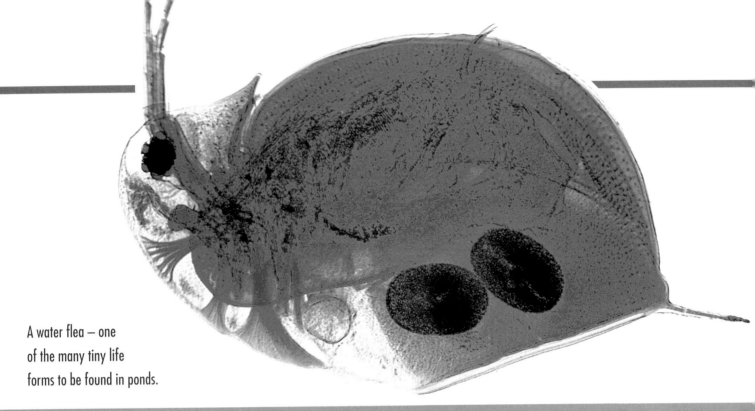

A water flea – one of the many tiny life forms to be found in ponds.

Put a little water in the dish and gently sweep the net through the pond water. Try not to stir up the mud. Gently tip the net out into the dish. Let the water settle and look carefully. Use a spoon or pipette to move any animals to a polythene bag with a little water. Tie the bag leaving plenty of air in it. You can examine these animals later with a magnifying glass and compare them to others you may find.

Repeat your pond dip. Use the small metal sieve to collect mud from the pond sides. Wash the mud carefully in a bucket of water to see if there are any larger creatures such as worms.

When working near water always take an adult with you or be very careful to only work in shallow water.

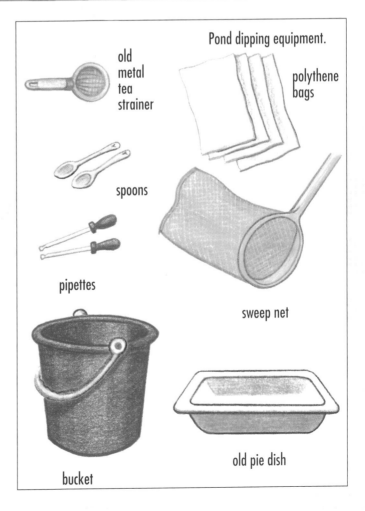

Pond dipping equipment.

old metal tea strainer

polythene bags

spoons

pipettes

sweep net

bucket

old pie dish

13

In and out of water

Can anything be more beautiful than the almost transparent, shining wings of the dragonfly? These insects visit many watery habitats and they rely on the water since it is here that the dragonfly lays her eggs. Many creatures spend part of their life away from water, but must return to breed.

Dragonfly eggs soon hatch and the larvae crawl out into the mud at the bottom of the pond. Some species spend years here, catching and eating small animals. When a larva is ready for a life in the air, it climbs up a plant stem. Above the water, the skin splits and the adult crawls out with its soft body and wings. Slowly, the fragile wings fill with liquid. They expand and allow the insect to fly.

Despite spending most of their lives on land, frogs and toads need water to breed. They are creatures belonging to the group of animals called amphibians. Large numbers of frogs or toads in northern Europe will sometimes hold up traffic as they cross roads on their way to ponds. There they will mate and each female will lay up to 4,000 eggs covered with a sticky jelly. This is the spawn. Tadpoles emerge after two or three weeks. They have gills to breathe underwater and soon feed on plants. When their first legs begin to grow six weeks later, they change their diet to meat. A small froglet will have grown after about three months and will soon emerge from the water for the first time – but it may be three years before it is a full-grown adult.

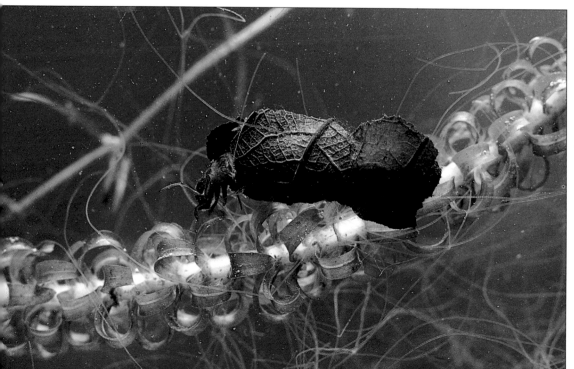

The larva of the caddis fly lives underwater and has a soft body — and some species build a special case for protection. This caddis larva lives in a case of leaves.

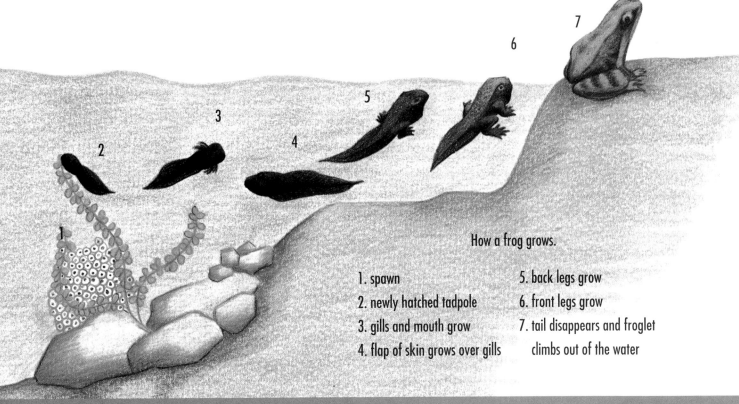

How a frog grows.

1. spawn
2. newly hatched tadpole
3. gills and mouth grow
4. flap of skin grows over gills
5. back legs grow
6. front legs grow
7. tail disappears and froglet climbs out of the water

REARING TADPOLES

In the spring, put water plants in the soil in an aquarium and fill it with water. Collect the sticky frogspawn from a pond with a net and place some in the aquarium.

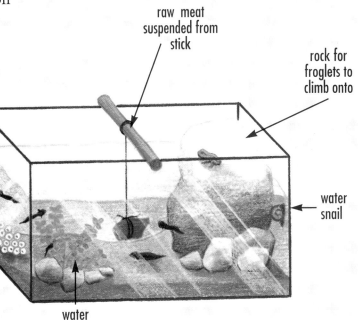

raw meat suspended from stick

rock for froglets to climb onto

water fleas

spawn

water snail

water plants

Carefully watch the spawn and draw how the spawn and the tadpoles change over the weeks. When their back legs begin to grow they will need to eat meat.

Collect some water fleas from the pond and add to the aquarium. Tie a small piece of raw meat to some string and suspend it in the water.

Make sure a rock is placed in the aquarium before the tadpoles' tails disappear so the froglets can climb out of the water. They are then ready to be released back into the pond.

Water wings

Many of the larger lakes in parks were designed with birds in mind. About 350 years ago, London's St James's Park was created for King James I, who was fascinated by birds. He brought eagles from Scotland and cormorants from the coast and in later years pelicans from the USA were added to the lake.

Your park lake is unlikely to have such an unusual collection, but you may have fascinating waterbirds. Ducks are the most usual town 'water wings' including the beautiful teal, widgeon, tufted duck and shoveler.

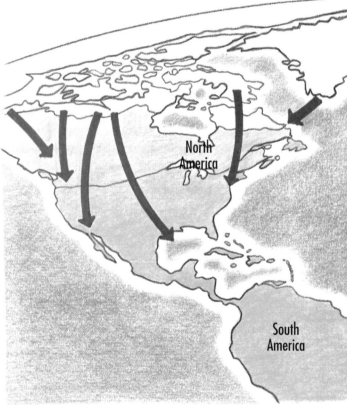

▲ Herons on the bank of a lake keeping their eyes open for fish.

Every winter millions of geese and swans fly south from the Arctic to warmer lands and lakes. ▶

A mute swan carrying its young cygnets. When afraid that its young are in danger, a swan will chase off an intruder. A beat of one of its powerful wings has been known to break a human arm!

The shoveler is a water bird that has a large, wide beak perfectly suited for feeding on the water's surface – it works like a sieve letting the water out and keeping the food in.

Arctic

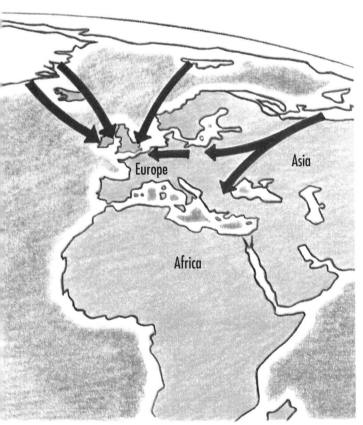

Europe

Asia

Africa

The swan has a different feeding technique: thrusting its head and long neck into the water to browse the plants. House martins, swallows and even bats are also attracted to the insects which collect over water. But too many birds cause problems. Their droppings can enrich the lake so much that huge growths of algae grow and poison the fish.

Even in summer, the far north of the Arctic is cold. It is here that many swans and geese breed. As the winter returns, ponds and lakes freeze over and it is time for the families to migrate. Massive flocks of these birds fly south: some from Canada fly to the USA, some from Scandinavia and Russia fly to the UK, the Netherlands and France. A single flock may contain 100 families, flying in a V-shape and honking loudly to one another. Many may spend the winter as wild tourists in your local lake, before setting off on their long flight back to the Arctic in the spring.

City grasslands

Our parks are the first places we think of when searching for wildlife in towns. But they are far more than just grass and trees...

When the first public parks were built during the last century they were intended as places for people to exercise and escape from the overcrowded streets. Parks may contain many different habitats, including shrubs, woodland, flower beds, but are mostly grass.

The grass is there to show off buildings, trees and flower beds, and for people to walk or lie on. It is easy to repair and look after, and is regularly mown and treated with chemicals. For these reasons, it can be something of a desert for wildlife, but even in a desert, there is life.

Most wild plants cannot grow with the regular mowing, but some, like the daisy, are low-lying and hug the ground – sometimes they escape the mower's blade. For most of the year the daisy produces flowers and so can reproduce.

The bush cricket will eat most plants, small animals and even discarded paper!

The daisy usually closes its petals at night, and so it got the name 'day's eye' – the time when it is open. Creeping thistle is another 'weed' which is difficult for gardeners to remove. It has a long underground root and if cut it will soon grow a new stem. Other wild plants will seize the opportunity to grow where the mower cannot reach – around trees and hedges or along walls.

Bush crickets also thrive more in parks than people's gardens, grazing in the longer grass and shrubs and making their characteristic chirping sound by rubbing their wings together. The regular mowing of grass is particularly helpful for some birds. Blackbirds can see earthworms more easily, and sparrows can find insects in the cut grass. In turn, hawks will be attracted to the park if they discover sparrows there.

▲ A fairy ring – a mysterious circle of fungi.

The blackbird is an expert wormer. ▼

DID YOU KNOW?

Fairy rings

Have you ever seen a fairy ring in your park? This is a circle of dark green in the grass – sometimes toadstools grow around the edge. This is not the work of fairies! Rather it is the result of a single tiny spore from a fungus sending out a network of tiny roots in all directions. The dark green circle shows its full size. If you find one, measure its diameter. Return the following year and see how much bigger it has grown.

In the gardens

A park's shrubs are extremely important for birds. They make good nesting sites and offer protection from predators and the weather. The blackbird, robin and song thrush especially nest in shrubs and hedges. In the centre of the British city of Leicester, starlings have chosen park shrubs to form the largest roost in Europe. More than one million starlings nest here, and unfortunately their droppings are killing large areas of the shrubs.

As soon as the park's flowers open in spring they are visited by countless insects. Tiny aphids feed on plants and are in turn harvested by ladybirds. Butterflies flit in and out of the gardens in search of nectar. Bumble bees, too, will visit flowers for nectar in the spring. These are the queen bees just woken from their winter sleep. They will soon find a nest, or excavate one underground, to lay eggs.

The queen's first offspring are worker bees and they spend their time collecting pollen and nectar from flowers including Californian lilac, willows, lime, apple and pear trees. They comb the pollen that sticks to their hairy bodies and put it in 'pollen baskets' on their back legs, but some pollen is brushed off onto other flowers, so the bees help to pollinate many plants and allow them to reproduce.

For bees, life in the city is much sweeter than in the country – where they are often killed by the chemicals put on crops and by a mite which attacks their blood stream. Many other species of bee visit our parks and gardens, including the honey bee. In the centre of London alone, there are about 500 bee-keepers looking after 5,000 colonies of bees. Each colony makes up to 80 kg of honey a year.

Parks – designed for people rather than wildlife.

Birds are usually welcomed in the park, but some species such as sparrows and pigeons often search for food in flower beds and trample on plants and bulbs emerging in the spring. This song thrush is raising her young in a park hedge.

PLANNING AN ECOLOGICAL PARK

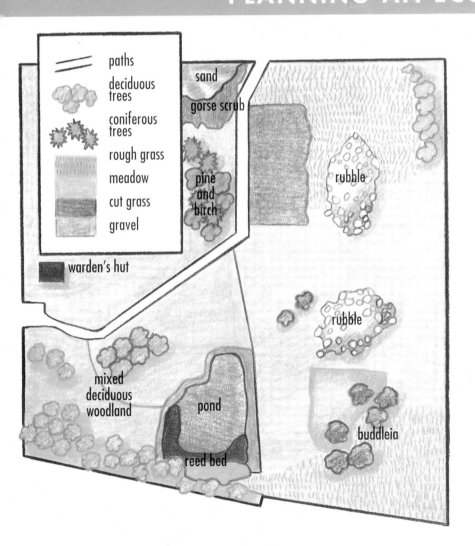

paths
deciduous trees
coniferous trees
rough grass
meadow
cut grass
gravel

warden's hut

sand
gorse scrub
pine and birch
rubble
rubble
mixed deciduous woodland
pond
reed bed
buddleia

Instead of being created purely for people, ecological parks are designed for wildlife and people in the heart of cities. In London, the Trust for Urban Ecology has created several such parks with different habitats including grassland, meadow, scrub, woodland and a pond. These attract a huge range of insects, mammals, frogs and birds including herons.

Visit your own town park and make a plan of how you would turn it into an ecological park.

21

Branching out

In a park you are likely to find the largest variety of trees in a town. Species that grow naturally in the area will support more life. Those that are introduced will be unfamiliar to the local insects, which will have to adapt if they want to live and feed on them.

Rhododendrons are very common in parks; their colourful blooms are beautiful, yet their leaves are acidic. This means that as they decay, the acid leaks into the surroundings and prevents snails from building up their shells, which need alkali conditions. The only benefit to wildlife from rhododendrons is that they produce tangled cover for thrushes, blackbirds and other nesting birds.

In Britain, the plane tree is typical of parks and is very resistant to air pollution. Its bark peels off and keeps the tree's breathing holes open. Birch trees are also planted in new parks, since they grow quickly and stand up to wind and cold.

From wildlife's point of view, a dead or dying tree is one of the most important parts of a woodland. It provides a home for fungi, ferns, mosses and beetles. The beetles in turn will be a delicacy for woodpeckers or some bats. Unfortunately, most dead and dying trees are thought to be an eyesore in parks and are cut down and taken away.

Turkey oak is a typical town tree often planted in public parks.

City parks usually contain a number of old, forest-size trees in which you may see nesting jays and magpies. You may also see birds that might never visit a smaller garden. If you hear a fast drumming noise, look out for a woodpecker clinging close to a tree. It chisels the bark with its bill up to 20 times per second, and then uses its long flexible tongue to catch insects. Even a lone oak tree has so many nooks and crannies that it is home to as many as 140 different species of insects.

Sometimes found in town parks, the lesser spotted woodpecker is the smallest European woodpecker.

INVESTIGATING TREES

Place a large white sheet underneath a low branch of a tree. Birch and oak trees are best. With a strong stick, hit the branch. Leaves will fall on to the sheet along with any animals.

Use plastic spoons or paint brushes to pick up the animals to examine them. Make a note of the number of each species you find.

Are there many caterpillars and spiders? What do you think each animal eats?

Return all animals to the tree when you have finished. Investigate other species of tree and compare your results.

Big game in the park

London's Richmond Park is home to about 600 deer.

For a grey squirrel a park must be heaven! There are trees for shelter and plenty of food, including tit-bits from humans. It may look cute as it begs for food, but the grey squirrel is a killer. A few squirrels were brought from the USA to Britain at the end of the last century and within a few years their numbers had grown to thousands. Too many squirrels cause problems in town parks. In winter, they kill trees by chewing the bark. In spring, they eat eggs, young birds and emerging flower buds.

Some larger parks have rabbits. Sometimes they have patchy marks on their fur suggesting that they have bred with tame rabbits which have escaped. Rats, voles, wood mice and shrews are also frequently seen in parks, but this is not their main habitat. Shrews eat huge numbers of insects and the smallest town-living mammals are the least shrew of the US and the pygmy shrew of Europe – just 50 mm long – plus a 40 mm tail!

To keep the grass short, some park keepers have brought in grazing animals. Sheep, cattle, ponies and deer are all used in town parks, but they require special things such as fencing, water and food during snowy weather.

Geese are grazing in a surprising number of city parks. If there is a lake in a park, there may be a thriving population of Canada geese, keeping the grass cropped short.

Of the largest mammals, only the deer that sometimes wander into a town remind us of the time when city and country were not so separated. All over the world, half-wild deer are kept in parks. There have been deer in London's royal parks since the time of King Henry VIII, and today there are more than a thousand.

▲ Living mowing-machines on the move.

▼ In some Australian city parks, koalas are sometimes found in eucalyptus trees.

DID YOU KNOW?

Big city deers
The world's largest deer is the elk. In Sweden there are around 300,000 elks. Occasionally small herds of elk wander from the forest at the edge of Stockholm, capital of Sweden, and follow the streets into the city centre, causing huge traffic jams. In Moscow, too, elk frequently wander into the city from the surrounding forest. Strangest of all is that sometimes swift-running white tailed deer get lost in New York city.

School environments

You don't always need special school trips to the country or nature reserves to find out about the natural world – interesting plants and animals will be in your school's backyard.

How good an environment is your school yard? The British organization, Learning Through Landscapes, made a study of 2,500 UK schools in 1994. It found that a third have between 20 and 50 trees, and a fifth of schools have more than 100 trees.

This is good news for creatures that live in trees, but what of the people who have to spend time in the grounds? A student spends about a quarter of a school day in a playground – an environment where animals can't live – on hard tarmac and concrete. But it doesn't have to be like this.

Learning Through Landscapes has helped 10,000 schools change their surroundings and make them better for plants, animals and young people. You could adopt a small area and ask permission to plant seeds or flowers to attract insects. A sheltered corner would be suitable for butterflies. A bird feeder hung from a pole or trees would give birds food all year round.

A pile of logs in a shaded area of soil will rot and encourage insects, fungi and mosses to colonize – and will attract birds looking for food. A pile of twigs near a tree makes a good nesting place for small mammals and birds – even a hibernating hedgehog or mouse in winter. A playing field is regularly mown and is not such a good habitat for wildlife, but let areas of surrounding grass grow tall, or see if wild grasses and flowers can be sown – different types for different areas.

At work collecting bugs in the long grass.

MAP YOUR SCHOOL GROUNDS

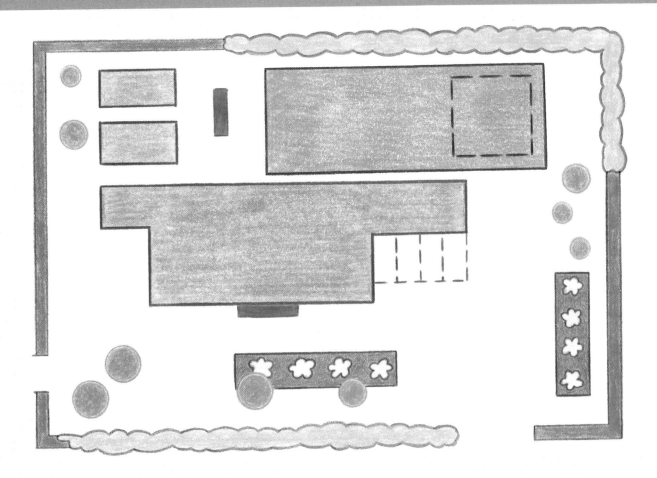

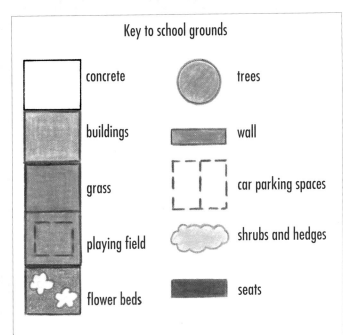

Key to school grounds

concrete		trees	
buildings		wall	
grass		car parking spaces	
playing field		shrubs and hedges	
flower beds		seats	

Just how many habitats and other features are there in your school grounds? Get to know this environment by walking round it and writing down the main habitats and the plants and animals you find in each.

Measure the size of your grounds and make a map of the habitats. Your school may already have a plan of the school grounds and you can add important areas to it. Are there overgrown or forgotten corners you could protect or improve for wildlife?

Act local

An overgrown area of ground can be turned into a wildlife garden with a pond.

Making the best of what you have in your school grounds is important for wildlife and it is possible to change the environment.

Students and teachers at thousands of schools have taken action to redesign their surroundings. At the Washington School in California, USA, pupils decided that their playground needed attention. The big ugly expanse of black concrete playground surrounded by a fence was divided into three parts.

The pupils redesigned the playground – one part was kept as a pavement for playing, one part was made into a maze with an area for wooden climbing equipment, the third part was turned into a nature garden.

In the nature garden, the pupils planted trees, flowers, wild grasses, and vegetables for food. They also dug two ponds. Eventually, the ugly chain fence was covered by climbing vines which flowered in the summer.

At Sutton Grammar School in Britain, students started a Conservation Club and were allowed to adopt an overgrown, unused piece of land in the school grounds. They decided to build a wildlife garden with a pond at the centre. Their first task was to organize a poster campaign asking people not to use the site as a litter dump.

The Club even raised the money to buy equipment and plants. Each Sunday afternoon, the Club met to carry out the hard work. The pond was filled with water, and plants such as lilies were introduced along with frogs and toadspawn. Finally a path was built around the garden so the whole school could use and enjoy it.

BUILDING A POND

Choose a site for your pond away from overhanging trees. Dig out your pond making sure it is at least 60 cm deep (so even in a cold winter the water in the bottom will not be frozen) and about 2 m across. Make the sides rough and sloping and build a shelf around the edge 25 cm deep and 25 cm wide. Remove sharp stones and sticks and line the pit with sand. Line the pit with tough plastic and hold down the edges with stones. Run water into the pit until full.

A shallow pond can have one or two large rocks in the middle as little islands for birds and water insects. Planting should be done in spring and summer.

Canadian pond weed can be added to float in the water. Water lilies and water milfoil can be planted in a flower pot of soil and placed on the shelf or bottom of the pond. Clumps of water violets can be put in nets with stones as weights and dropped on to the shelf.

Filling the pond with water.

Life on the line

Roads, railway lines and canals – corridors for human communication – are essential habitats in which non-human life can thrive.

When they were first built, the railways in most countries changed the way people lived. They allowed more people to move around between town and country, and brought new industries. They also had an effect on the spread of plants. The tiny seeds of flowering plants and the spores of ferns can travel long distances, pulled along by the air of a passing train, or hitching a lift inside a carriage. Insects, too, can be blown, especially baby money spiders. They produce a long thread of silk which is rather like a tiny kite. When a gust of wind catches it, the spider is blown – sometimes for huge distances. The draught from a train is more than enough to take a small spider from one station to the next.

The plant life of railway verges attract rabbits – each rabbit needs 0·5 kg of greens to eat a day.

As well as for plants, railway lines are green corridors for foxes and rabbits to enter the heart of our cities. Here, railway tracks, sidings, depots and verges provide many habitats. In the UK there are more than 4,000 km of track in towns and cities. Some are so important for wildlife that they are specially protected areas.

A lizard has made the railway line its home.

As towns have expanded and farmers have changed their methods, certain countryside habitats have disappeared, and many plants have become very rare. Railway embankments are difficult and dangerous to get to. However, they provide a priceless undisturbed habitat for many rare plants. And these in turn are host to many small animals, especially insects such as butterflies.

The dry banks and gravel alongside the tracks make ideal sun-bathing areas for snakes and lizards. Wood mice, voles, brown rats and rabbits will also make their homes on railway embankments. In turn, rabbits and voles provide meals for the foxes which dig holes and rear their young metres away from the thundering trains.

DID YOU KNOW?

A hitch-hiking flower

Oxford ragwort was first found growing on the slopes of a volcano in Italy, and taken to England more than 200 years ago. Planted in the Botanic Garden in Oxford, its seeds escaped on the wind and in 1879 it was found growing near the new train station 2 km away. Passing trains blew seeds along the track and in a few years plants were growing in London, more than 80 km away. Eventually they spread to most parts of the UK.

Brown rats flourish in the quiet nooks and crannies of disused railway stations and embankments.

GREEN CORRIDORS

Roads and pavements

How much of your town is taken up by roads, pavements and footpaths? Up to one-third of a town's area is devoted to these. In towns, roads are designed for vehicle drivers to see well, and for people to get from one place to another. Wildlife is not considered when roads are planned, but even a small group of plants and animals on a grassy verge will have their own ecology.

Only around one-third of European town roads are designed to have a grass verge.

These verges are often trampled and mowing and the use of chemicals to kill weeds does not make them an important site for wildlife. Yet verges on steep slopes where mowing is difficult can have many wild grasses and weeds to attract insects.

Out of the town, alongside motorways, the grass is allowed to grow longer and provides an important haven for wild flowers, insects and small mammals. Kestrels will often be seen 'hovering' alongside motorways, preparing to dive on a vole or mouse.

The trees and shrubs planted around this US business park and nearby freeway are an important environment for wildlife.

Plane trees, resistant to pollution, flourish close to busy city streets providing a sanctuary for a host of birds and insects.

In cities around the world, trees grow alone or in small groups along the roadsides. Lime, sycamore, beech and plane trees grace London's streets, while redwoods and Ponderosa pines are found in San Francisco, horse chestnuts in Paris, and aspens, elms and 'tree of heavens' in New York.

In summer, up to a million tiny insects – lime aphids – feed on the sugary liquid in the leaves of each lime tree. They drop the sugar they don't need to the ground, often covering parked cars. Ash trees are prone to their trunks swelling, which lifts kerbstones out of line. Poplars have long roots which can damage walls. All can grow and break sewers and other underground pipes.

Tragedy for this elk is also the magpies' good fortune.

DID YOU KNOW?

Death on the roads

The number of animals killed each year on British roads may be around one million. Rabbits, foxes, squirrels, pigeons and sparrows suffer particularly badly. Squashed hedgehogs, frogs and rats are also seen in towns. Black cats are anything but lucky. One scientist studying cat deaths on town roads found that 60 per cent of all casualties were black. Remember, however, that a large number of dead animals reflects a thriving population in the area.

Waterways

Wildlife, safe from road traffic, flourishes on canals and old docks which pass through many towns. The canals in northern Europe were built more than 200 years ago to link the new factories and mills with the raw materials they needed, and to transport finished goods to the growing towns and cities. At first, the longboats were pulled by horses. Soon, however, the railways took over as the best way of transporting goods and people.

Canals have turned many rivers into a web of waterways. With their use as highways, species have been able to spread across countries. Canadian pond weed was accidentally brought from North America to Britain in 1848, attached to logs. Some 30 years later, it had grown so wildly that it was a danger to river traffic, and through the canal system it had begun to spread around the country. From the USA, more pond weeds and water snails were brought by accident. Factories which empty warm waste water into canals help to raise the canal temperature to that which these new species are used to. And there have even been cases of unusual tropical fish – released from pet shops – living and breeding in canals near to these warm water outlets.

Half of all British people live within 8 km of a canal.

Canals are like long, narrow ponds, and usually have slow-moving water. Plenty of boat traffic will prevent most underwater plants getting a hold. But unused canals will fill up with plant life and turn it into a marsh – ideal places for dragonflies.

Canals are important sites for waterbirds to rear their young. ➤

The number of water voles in the UK is falling, but humans are placing pipes in the banks of many canals to encourage voles to set up home and breed. ▼

Many of the fish and birds of canals are those you would expect in a pond, especially the white-beaked coots and red-beaked moorhens which hide in the rushes and reeds. Those patient anglers, kingfishers and herons, are gradually moving closer to towns, following the path of the canals. In the heart of busy Amsterdam, herons are not unusual sights, standing by the famous canals.

Water voles and water shrews are at home in canals. The water vole usually digs two holes in the bank, one above the other. The top hole is the entrance to the winter home, since with the greater flow of water in winter the summer home gets flooded. Inside, a system of tunnels links sleeping quarters and a nursery for the young.

35

Quiet churchyards

The quiet of a churchyard – ideal for wildlife.

Even in the middle of a concrete desert you can find oases of greenery and wildlife.

Cemeteries vary from enormous suburban graveyards to small city-centre churchyards. Unlike parks, churchyards are quiet and often surrounded by old trees and bushes – a sheltered home for rabbits and squirrels, and in North America skunks and opossums. It has even been known for a family of chipmunks to hibernate through the winter inside an old tomb.

In British churchyards, yew trees are common and can live for up to 1,000 years, providing a home for generations of birds such as jays and goldcrests. Bats, swifts and some owls will find a home inside or on the church itself, while lizards will bask on the sunny walls of Mediterranean churches. Wood mice are woodland animals now living happily among the trees in churchyards, nimbly climbing bark and branches, and digging complex underground tunnels. Shrews are fierce hunters of worms and beetles, and live among the dead leaves or take over the tunnels of wood mice. In turn, foxes and owls will come in search of the small mammals. Tawny owls will nest in British churchyards, while in the USA the whistle of the screech-owl can sometimes be heard in graveyards.

Because of the age of many churches, very old and rare lichens may be found growing in a crust on tombstones. The importance of graveyards to wildlife is now being recognized. The American Nature Conservancy group has turned an old Californian churchyard into a wildflower reserve. In London, run-down cemeteries are preserved for their richness of wild flowers and grasses, and many have turned to woodland.

A skunk hiding in a woody US cemetery.

Life after death — bluebells and lichen thrive on an old grave.

Churchyard sancturies

As towns grow into cities, they often surround small villages and their old churches. Sometimes, the trees in churchyards will be older than the city itself, and captured in the churchyard will be the remains of the woodland or meadows that stood before the city was built. In England and Wales (an area of 150,000 km^2) there are 40,000 churchyards – and a quarter of them are at least 500 years old. These churchyards make up a huge wildlife reserve.

The wood mouse is a woodland animal happily living in the green of churchyards. ▼

Wastelands

Wastelands and vacant lots are a major feature of cities, particularly the inner areas of industrial towns. Sometimes these are places where houses or factories are knocked down. The sites may be grassed over or built on again; often they are simply left. But they are not empty for long – nature quickly moves in.

It is possible to work out how long an area has been left vacant by looking at the species of plants. Over time, plants develop in a series of stages sometimes ending up with scrub woodland.

This is called plant succession. After demolition and the removal of the rubble, light seeds blown on the wind arrive. Oxford ragwort is typical, so too are buddleia and willowherbs. Wheat seeds may be brought by birds and accidentally dropped. Humans dumping rubbish can bring potatoes which grow plants.

Wasteland sometimes turns into a forest of young trees quite soon, but their space is soon crowded out by herbs. After three or four years, if the site is undisturbed, tall leafy plants like rosebay willowherb dominate. First rosebay spreads by wind blowing its seeds, then it grows underground stems which produce buds and new plants. These underground stems can grow up to 1 m a year. Michelmas daisy and lupin are other tall herbs which may be common.

Life will bloom almost anywhere – even in a desert of rubble.

With time, the amount of grass in the site increases, so that after ten years the wasteland may become grassland with tall patches of herbs. The large seeds of trees like ash, sycamore and laburnum may be blown into the wasteland – but only if there are parent trees near. Elder, hawthorn and apple tree seeds are brought in by birds. They grow very quickly and if undisturbed the area becomes a woodland, quite unlike anything found elsewhere. Wastelands are true town environments.

Herbs such as rosebay soon dominate wasteland.

STUDY AN URBAN WASTELAND

Hammer two stakes in the ground, about 5 or 6 m apart. Stretch a long piece of string along the ground and tie to each stake. Slowly work your way from one stake to the other looking at the plant and animal life. Measure the distance along the string where you find each one, draw pictures of them or write down the name of the species. Repeat this for different parts of the site: along a wall, over a ditch, fallen tree or burnt ground. How do the areas compare? How did the plant and animal life get there?

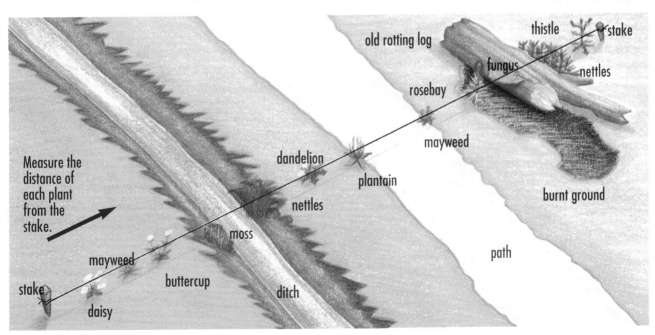

Rubble invaders

Plants on wastelands are only half the story. Animals soon find their way to new sites. First on the scene are winged creatures – birds, butterflies, moths and some beetles, as well as money spiders, blown in on the breeze like kites. In this barren landscape, species will often cluster around a single plant for food and shelter.

As the plants change through succession, so do the animals. As the site gets older, insects which feed on a wide range of plants are replaced by those which feed on a just a few species. After two or three years, plants will have died and their decaying remains will feed more life. As the site becomes damper, woodlice, slugs, millipedes and centipedes will move in. Woodlice and ground beetles like to live in soil full of cracks and crannies, but after several years the plants have grown roots filling up the spaces between the rubble. Woodlice and beetles may then be less common, and earthworms and ants become more widespread.

Walk across a grassy city wasteland on a hot summer's day and you may disturb many grasshoppers – the air will be full of their chirping. They need only a small amount of grassland to survive and so rapidly invade wastelands.

Wherever there is grassland, grasshoppers will be attracted.

As the site gets older and a thick covering of grass grows, voles may make their home. Old bottles left on sites are frequently a death trap for mice and insects alike. Once inside in search of water they cannot get out through the slippery glass slides. Brown rats also may find refuge in wastelands, particularly when their factory home is demolished.

A rosebay willowherb has an elephant hawkmoth caterpiller as a guest.

ADOPT A WASTELAND

There may be a piece of wasteland near you to adopt. Someone, somewhere may own the site, so it is best to write to the town council for help in finding the owner. Some councils even give money to help people turn wastelands into nature gardens!

Remove most of the metal waste and all the plastic, but don't tidy up too much. Use climbing plants to cover junk. Nettles and other weeds can be dug up from gardens and planted on the site. Rubble can be used to form mini-beast habitats.

sign explains to passing people

Wildlife Lives Here!

unwanted plants from the garden add nectar and seeds

rubble habitat for mini-beasts

plants grow to cover junk

a neat edging makes a site look attractive

Night wings

Many species only come out under cover of the dark. For them, this is their best time to find food – they are nocturnal.

By dusk in the summer there are hundreds of moths flitting through parks, gardens and wasteland in search of food or a mate. Most are attracted to bright lights and if you leave a window open with the light on you will also be inviting dozens of moths and hundreds of tiny flies including gnats and midges.

Bats mostly eat flying insects, and catch their food on the wing, finding their prey with their echo-location. Large industrial cities tend not to have enough insects to support many bat colonies, but they are common in

A privet hawk moth is the largest night-flying insect in the UK – it has a wing-span of 10 cm.

smaller towns. Bats are the only mammals that can power their own flight, having developed a skin of wings between their front and rear legs. Other mammals have developed similar flaps of skin, but they cannot fly, although the flying squirrel of the USA glides up to 30 m between park trees at night. In eastern Australia, the sugar glider is a possum gliding up to 60 m among the tree tops where it catches roosting birds, but its favourite food is the witchetty grub – the larva of the longhorn beetle.

The pipistrelle bat may be small but it has a big appetite – it needs to eat 3,000 insects a night.

Most owls are nocturnal. They live by the kill, and find plenty of food in towns. In the countryside owls eat small mammals, but in the city many owls have had to change their diet. Some eat nothing but sparrows and the occasional earthworm, large insects, or even fish from a pond.

The tawny owl is a frequent visitor to European towns and cities. It hunts for rodents in gardens and parks.

ATTRACTING MOTHS

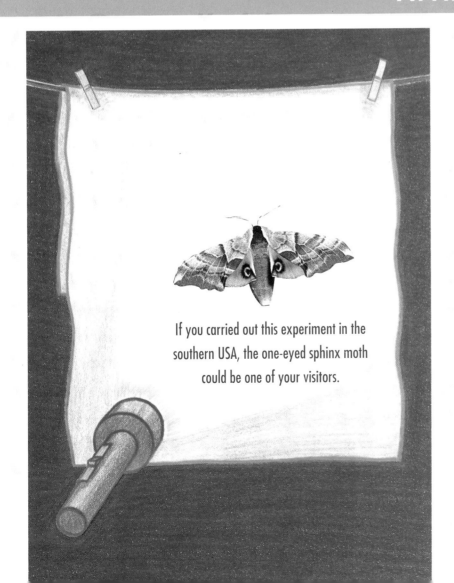

If you carried out this experiment in the southern USA, the one-eyed sphinx moth could be one of your visitors.

Choose a dry, fine night with little wind and wait until it is quite dark. Hang a large white sheet over a washing line and position one or two powerful torches or lamps so they shine on the sheet. Alternatively, place the sheet on the ground with the lamp on it. Moths will flit towards the sheet and settle on flowers to feed.

Take a close look at a feeding moth with a torch and magnifying glass. If you leave your light on and curtains undrawn many will settle on your window.

Night stalkers

The park gates are shut; the humans have gone. The fox has a free run. It has full garbage bins to scavenge, ducks asleep near a pond to creep up on, rats to be chased and even earthworms to be dug up. While we sleep through the night, the town is alive with life, particularly hunters such as foxes. Foxes make homes and raise cubs in suburban gardens and parks in US and European cities. One even made a home under a stand in the famous US Yankee Stadium.

Unusual inhabitants of cities in the USA are coyotes. Although normally found in prairies, they have now taken up residence in cities as different as Chicago and Denver.

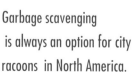

Garbage scavenging is always an option for city racoons in North America.

Badgers searching for food scraps in a suburban garden in the UK.

About the same size as the fox, the pretty-faced racoon is an expert climber in US cities and will take birds and eggs, but prefers frogs and fish which it will take from ponds. Stoats and weasels are seen in larger parks at night stalking rabbits, mice, voles and small birds. In North America the larger long-tailed weasel occasionally visits gardens and parks along with mink, which perhaps hunt the small vole-like muskrat.

After a night feasting on beetles, caterpillars and earthworms, a hedgehog looks for a place to sleep.

The badger is a true nocturnal animal and has made its home on the edges of British towns, near canals, wastelands and railway lines. In adapting to town life, the badger has needed to change its behaviour. The underground home, or set, it excavates is smaller than in the countryside, and it emerges later at night since towns can still be noisy places well after dark.

A most unusual night time visitor to suburban gardens in southern USA is the Texas armadillo. It is the only mammal to have strong armour protecting its body – and it can roll up into an armoured ball for self-defence. Its long tongue collects ants and termites along with the occasional snail.

Our left-overs are a fox's evening meal.

Glossary

Adapt To change and adjust to the environment.

Algae A major group of simple plants without stems, roots and leaves.

Amphibians Cold blooded animals which live on land but needing water to breed. Amphibians include frogs, toads and newts.

Colonize To slowly become established in a place.

Ecology The study of how living things affect each other, and how they are affected by their environment.

Elk The largest deer in Europe.

Environment Everything, both living and non-living, that surrounds and affects a life form.

Feral Wild.

Hibernate A kind of deep sleep when an animal's functions slow down to survive times of cold.

Larva Some creatures such as insects undergo great changes as they grow from egg to adult. A larva emerges from an egg and sheds its skin several times to allow for growth. Grubs (for beetles), maggots (for flies) and caterpillars (for butterflies) are all larvae.

Lichen Slow- growing, coloured, growths on rocks and walls – made up of fungus and algae living together and benefiting from each other.

Migrate To travel long distances to a new home at a regular time each year.

Nocturnal Active mostly at night.

Nutrients Essential substances found in soil and water which plants need to produce their food.

Pollen The powder produced by a flowering plant necessary for reproduction.

Pollination The movement of pollen from one part of a plant to another so that it may reproduce.

Pupa The stage in a creature's development between larva and adult.

Species The name given to the smallest grouping or 'type' of plant and animal. There are believed to be about 30 million different species on the Earth.

Spore Rather like a tiny seed, these are produced by some plants and will grow into a new plant if conditions are right.

Succession The way that the mix of plants colonizing wasteland changes in stages over time.

Resources

Organizations to contact

United Kingdom

British Trust for Conservation
Volunteers
36 St Mary's Street, Wallingford
Oxfordshire OX10 0EU

Butterfly Conservation
PO Box 222, Dedham
Essex CO7 6EY

Centre of the Earth
42 Norman Street, Winson Green
Birmingham B18 7EP

Churchyard Discovery Project
Bristol Wildlife Centre
Jacobs Wells Road, Bristol BS8 1DR

Council for Environmental
Education, University of Reading
Reading RG1 5AQ

Crest, Surrey Technology Centre
University of Surrey
Guildford GU2 5YH

Learning Through Landscapes
Southside Offices, The Law Courts
Winchester SO23 9DL

London Ecology Unit
Bedford House
125 Camden High Street
London NW1 7JR

National Children's Play and
Recreation Centre
359-361 Euston Road
London NW1 3AL

RSPB, The Lodge, Sandy
Bedfordshire SG19 2DL

Tree Council, 35 Belgrave Square
London SW1X 8QN

Trust for Urban Ecology
PO Box 514, London SE16 1AS

Urban Wildlife Groups
for your local group contact:
RSNC, 22 The Green, Nettleham
Lincoln LN2 2NR

Australia

Australian Association for
Environmental Education
GPO Box 112, Canberra, ACT 2601

Canada

Canadian Museum of Nature
PO Box 3443, Station D
Ottawa K1P 6P4

New Zealand

Environmental and Conservation
Organizations of New Zealand
PO Box 11057
Wellington

Books to read

Chris Baines, *The Wild Side of Town*,
BBC Books, 1986
Michael Chinery, *Parks and Gardens*,
Kingfisher, 1985
Michael Chinery, *Wildlife in Towns and
Cities*, Country Life Books, 1985
Jennifer Cochrane, *Urban Ecology*,
Wayland, 1987
The Earth Works Group, *50 Simple
Things Kids Can Do to Save the Earth*,
Sphere, 1990.
Ron Freethy, *Wildlife in Towns*,
Crowood Press, 1986
Ken Hoy, *Junior Naturalist in the Town*,
Guild, 1985
Dick King-Smith, *Town Watch*,
Puffin, 1987
Nature Areas for City People, London
Ecology Unit, 1990
Wildlife on Your Doorstep,
Reader's Digest, 1986
The Living Churchyard, RSNC, 1991
John Stevens, *The National Trust Book
of Wildflower Gardening*,
Dorling Kindersley, 1987

Videos/multimedia

Audubon's Backyard Birding, Philips
CD-I/National Audubon Society, 1994
Gardening With Wildlife Video,
RSPB, 1984
The Video Guide to Garden Birds,
RSPB/BBC, 1989
My World 2 – The Garden, Semerc, 1991

R E F E R E N C E

Index